DIVINE GUIDING LIGHT

Unveiling Islam's Message and

Your True Purpose of Life

THE SINCERE SEEKER COLLECTION

In the grand journey of life, as we are born into this world, we find ourselves seeking answers to profound questions that plague the conscience and inner thoughts of each of us: How did I get here? Why am I here? What's my life purpose? Where am I headed after I die?

You are driven to uncover these deep questions, and if you don't have the answers, a sense of unease lingers over you like a puzzle with missing pieces. You feel a void in your heart, and this feeling continues to weigh on you, making it difficult to live a content, peaceful life until you fill the void.

You were created with a predisposition to search for the purpose of life and bridge the empty gap in your heart. This predisposition is woven into your very nature; if it is not filled, you will feel empty, restless, lost, and alone in this world.

The human intellect alone cannot answer these questions unaided. You need Divine guidance to discover these all-important spiritual answers, the kind that only the One who created you can give. Only He can provide you with the purpose of your existence and provide the guidance needed to fulfill that purpose. Your Creator has given you a manual of your life and existence to bring clarity to everything, just as a maker of an electronic device encloses a user's manual that teaches how to operate the machine efficiently.

This life manual contains the verbatim word of God, meant for you to read, learn from, and live your life under its guidance. Known as Revelation, it was sent to you from above, from God Himself. He delivered it via an Angel who conveyed it to a human prophet, who then transmitted it to you and all of us. You cannot lead a life of tranquility or live a successful life without religion, and this religion cannot be a product of human creation. A true religion must be inherently Divine, free from human alterations.

God has sent thousands of prophets and messengers to humanity to convey His message and communicate with His creation. Every nation on Earth has received a prophet for this purpose. They all preached the same general message: only one God is worthy of worship. He is the One and Only God, without a partner, son, daughter, or equal. We should follow His commandments. These prophets were sent to steer their people away from worshipping created beings and toward worshipping the Creator of all things.

The prophets taught their people about the identity of their Creator, how to build a relationship with Him, and how to love Him. They also taught their people about the purpose of life and how to live a successful one in this world and the next. The prophets taught their people that life is a test, and those who pass it will be rewarded with paradise eternally, while those who fail will be punished in the hereafter.

When God's prophets departed, their people would distort the God-given Revelations they brought by adding and subtracting to the text and wrongly attributing them to God. What originated as pure Revelation from God became tainted with human words for their own gain.

As an extension of God's mercy and love, He would send another Messenger and Book to restore His Message and guide humanity back to Him whenever God's Revelation would get distorted. Prophet Moses (PBUH) was sent to the nation preceding us, the children of Israel.

Following his passing, the Revelation he bore was altered by people attributing their own writings to the divine words.

In response, God sent Jesus Christ to reinstate the divine message. After the departure of Prophet Jesus (PBUH) from this world, the message underwent distortion once more. So, God sent down His final Messenger with His final Revelation to the last nation: our own. God selected a man named Muhammad (PBUH), who resided in Arabia, to deliver His ultimate Revelation, which contained His verbatim words to humanity meant for both you and me.

This time, God did not rely on anyone to safeguard and maintain His final Revelation, the Glorious Quran, as He had entrusted scholars and Rabbis of past nations with the responsibility for preserving their Scriptures, which they ultimately failed to do. God undertook the duty Himself to protect, preserve, and uphold His ultimate Revelation to humanity. Since this would be the last Book for humanity, its preservation was paramount, ensuring it remained uncorrupted. Presently, the Glorious Quran remains unaltered, just as it was delivered over 1400 years ago, with each word and letter intact, as God had promised to preserve it for all of us.

The prior Messengers and Scriptures before the Glorious Quran and Prophet Muhammad (PBUH) were intended solely for specific groups within past nations. Prophets Moses and Jesus PBUT and the Scriptures they brought—the Torah and Gospel—were designated for their respective communities, not for us. Hence, God did not need to preserve their Scriptures for our benefit, as these teachings were not directed toward us, and these original Scriptures are now lost.

The present-day Bible and Torah differ from the original Revelations associated with Prophets Moses and Jesus (PBUT). They are products of anonymous authors and do not represent God's words or the Prophets. The discrepancies and contradictions within them serve as evidence of this fact.

Individuals contemplating God conjure up varying concepts or notions about Him. Some envision a bearded figure in the sky, while others imagine a being adorned with a blue hue, possessing four arms and a regal crown. These mental images are influenced by an individual's background, upbringing, and beliefs. So, what constitutes the Islamic understanding of God?

The Islamic perception of God, referred to as "Allah," is not exclusive to Muslims or Arabs alone. The Islamic concept of God encompasses the Creator of everything within the Heavens and Earth. "Allah" is merely the Arabic term for God.

Allah describes himself in the Glorious Quran in Chapter 112, saying:

**"Say, 'He is Allah, who is One, Allah, the Sustainer.
He neither begets nor is born, nor is there to Him any
equivalent.'" (Quran 112:1-4).**

Pause momentarily to acquaint yourself with the One who has created and fashioned you. Allah is One, He is unique, He is indivisible, He is Absolute. He has always existed without a start and will always be there without an end. Allah is self-sufficient; He does not need anything or anyone since He possess everything already, but everyone and everything needs Him.

God does not beget. He has no sons or daughters, partners or equals; nor is he begotten. He does not have parents. Allah is neither a man nor a woman nor a male or female. He transcends such classifications. Man, woman, male, female—all these categories are creations of God, whereas He stands beyond all such definitions. Comparing God to anything within human comprehension falls short, for God is unlike any experience or phenomenon we've encountered.

Allah has the most magnificent Names and Sublime perfect attributes. **"And to Allah belong the best names, so invoke Him by**

4

them" **(Quran 7:180)**. God is Perfect. He is the Most-High, the Most-Supreme. God is All-Powerful, having full authority over all things. He has no limitations. **"Whenever We will anything to be, We say unto it Our word "Be," and it is." (Quran 16:40)**. God is All-Knowing; All-Seeing. All-Hearing: nothing is hidden from Him. He encompasses all things: the open and the secret, the public and the private. **"Not a leaf falls but that He knows it. And no grain is there within the darkness of the earth and no moist or dry thing but that it is written in a clear record." (Quran 6:59)**

God is the Originator of the heavens and the Earth; He brought everything from mere nothingness into existence. **"He is Creator of the Heavens and the Earth. He has made for you from yourselves, mates, and among the cattle, mates; He multiplies you thereby. There is nothing like unto Him, and He is the Hearing, the Seeing." (Quran 42:11).** God is the Bestower of life and the Bringer of death. He holds authority on the Day of Judgment.

God is the Beneficent, most loving, most compassionate, and most merciful. He is the answerer of prayers and is involved and concerned with the daily affairs of all human beings. He is the One that accepts repentance from his servants and forgives all sins. Allah knows what you endure and understands your feelings and struggles. Allah understands because He has been there with you all along.

Allah is worthy of worship. None have the right to be worshipped but Him alone. No other being carries the right to be worshipped, revered, adored, invoked, supplicated, or shown any act of worship but Allah alone. He is the true God, and every other deity is false.

Moreover, God is All-Just. Consequently, wrongdoers and transgressors must be held accountable for their deeds. God is pure, righteous, and equitable. Allowing wrongdoing to go unpunished would be allowing evil to thrive unchecked. Since God would not allow that to happen, God's justice necessitates a fitting punishment for sinful actions from those who do not cease and repent. While Allah is not answerable to anyone, He has promised to act fairly toward all. God reigns above the heavens and His Throne, outside his creation, not confined by any physical dimension.

A wise, perfect, flawless being would not engage in creating human beings without intention, reason, or purpose. Such an action would possess a flaw, contradicting the nature of a perfect being devoid of imperfections. When you observe the Universe and all that it contains, you'll discern meticulous order, intelligence, design, and purpose. Consider the sun, which radiates light, warmth, and energy. Given the purpose infused into everything around you, why would you not assume that you, too, were created with a purpose?

Your life's purpose has been bestowed upon you by your Creator, transmitted through the conduit of Revelation by your Prophet. Your ultimate purpose is to connect with God, nurture a relationship with Him, and consistently struggle and submit to His divine will. The pinnacle of joy and tranquility you can attain in this world emanates from serving your Creator. Striving to be a devoted servant of God is paramount. God unequivocally proclaims that humankind was created to worship Him:

"And I did not create the jinn and mankind except to worship Me." (Quran 51:56)

It's important not to misconstrue this message to mean that God expects you to remain in perpetual prayer, endlessly immersed in His remembrance, and live a life of constant solitude and unceasing meditation. This interpretation is inaccurate. Worshiping God encompasses every belief, utterance, action and sentiment of the heart that aligns with God's approval and love. The concept of worship spans a comprehensive range of activities and sentiments.

However, this doesn't imply that you're free to worship God in any manner as you see fit. God and His Prophet, Muhammad (PBUH), have provided you with guidance on how to worship God and adhere to His commandments—fulfilling what He has ordained and abstaining from what He has prohibited.

As a Muslim, you will not merely live to fulfill your desires, impulses, and cravings. Instead, you will live in accordance with the guidance of your Creator. He alone comprehends what is best for you and what is not. Thus, you embrace His guidance and direction.

Islam isn't confined to rituals and traditions like prayer and fasting. It constitutes a comprehensive way of life that offers guidance for every facet. Islam teaches the art of living and dictates how you should steer and navigate your life. Islam instructs you about the things in this life that are beneficial to you and those that are ultimately destructive and should be avoided.

According to Islam, everyday human actions—eating, drinking, interacting, learning, dressing, resting, and acts of charity—can all be considered acts of worship where you'd be rewarded for if performed solely for God and aligned with His divine laws and guidelines.

The individual who submits to God's will and follows His guidance is referred to as a Muslim. By definition, a Muslim is one who surrenders their will to the Almighty God. This act of surrender is called "Islam" in Arabic, signifying submission or surrender to the Creator who brought you into existence— just as everything in nature around you.

Only when you submit to God, by believing in Him and obeying His directives, do you attain an inherent and enduring sense of security, genuine peace of mind, and assurance in your heart. You are submitting and worshipping the very same God whom all the preceding Prophets of God—Adam, Noah, Abraham, Joseph, Moses, David, Solomon, Jesus, and Prophet Muhammad (PBUT)—also worshipped and submitted to.

Contrary to popular misconception, Islam is not a recently emerged religion from the 7th century; it has existed since humanity's inception. Islam stands as the sole religion that God has commanded humanity to follow and the only religion acceptable by God. The last Prophet of humanity, Prophet Muhammad (PBUH), was not the originator of Islam, contrary to the common misconception. Instead, he was the final Prophet, dispatched by the Almighty to relay His message to us. Islam signifies the continuation, culmination, completion, and fulfillment of God's eternal and universal message to humanity, as revealed through all preceding Messengers and Prophets.

Throughout history, anyone who practiced monotheism by yielding to God's will and following their respective Prophet was recognized as a Muslim. Humans have been practicing Islam ever since the time of Prophet Adam (PBUH).

Yet, how can we attain certainty regarding the authenticity of Prophet Muhammad (PBUH) as an authentic prophet, the truthfulness of the Glorious Quran as the genuine word of God, and the legitimacy of Islam as a divinely ordained way of life and religion?

All of God's Prophets were provided with miracles, extraordinary acts that deviate from the laws of nature executed through divine intervention and intended to validate they were indeed sent from above as Prophets. The specific miracles they came with were crafted to resonate with what that nation excelled in, enhancing their understanding and persuasiveness rather than being dismissed as mere optical illusions.

For instance, consider the people of Egypt, who excelled in magic and sorcery and often interacted with spirits known as Jinn to conjure illusions. In response, God granted Prophet Moses (PBUH) miracles rooted in illusions, such as his staff transforming into a snake before his people's eyes and parting the Red Sea. These miracles aimed to substantiate his prophethood, humble his people, and remind them that the true power, dominion, and might reside with God.

Similarly, during the era of Prophet Jesus (PBUH), his people boasted of their advancements in medicine, healing, and the prowess of their doctors. Consequently, God sent Prophet Jesus (PBUH) with miracles that pertained to healing and surpassing the limits of medical science. These miracles encompassed the miraculous birth of Jesus (PBUH) from a virgin and his ability to heal lepers, restore sight to the blind, and resurrect the deceased—all through the will and permission of God.

These miracles demonstrated God's power, authenticated the Prophets' missions, and provided indisputable proof of their divine appointment. In the era of Prophet Muhammad (PBUH), God provided a distinct miracle to validate his prophethood—testifying that he was God's chosen messenger.

During that time, the Arabs, while predominantly illiterate, excelled in the spoken word. They were renowned for their eloquence and linguistic prowess, with their poetry and oral traditions serving as exemplars of literary excellence. The spoken word held immense value in their culture. Thus, God bestowed upon the final nation the ultimate masterpiece of eloquence and speech—the Glorious Quran. Its eloquence, imagery, and terms left the people of Prophet Muhammad (PBUH) awestruck. The Revelation of the Glorious Quran to an unlettered Prophet who could not read, write, or calculate served as conclusive evidence that he was not the author.

The Glorious Quran remains accessible to everyone across generations, enduring until the end of time. This miracle's power to convince, persuade, compel, and remain pertinent is as strong today as it was over 1400 years ago. As the ultimate Book for all humanity, it was destined to outlast Prophet Muhammad (PBUH) for future generations. Millions of people, from the time of its Revelation, have witnessed and embraced its divine nature, captivated by its remarkable style, content, and spiritual elevation.

Numerous compelling reasons substantiate the conviction that Islam is the divine religion, and the Glorious Quran represents the authentic word of God. If you are still unsure, you should investigate the evidence that validates these claims.

Amongst the many proofs of Islam's truthfulness is its alignment with the innate beliefs and predispositions God instilled within every human heart. Take, for instance, the concept of God. Islam's portrayal of God is straightforward, comprehensible, and less intricate than other religions. The notion of salvation—escaping hellfire and attaining paradise in the afterlife—coherently aligns with genuine justice. This contrasts with Christianity, where salvation supposedly hinges solely on belief in Jesus Christ's sacrifice, without necessitating any personal action for salvation. Islam maintains that salvation requires faith in the Creator, coupled with the correct intention, actions, and repentance. Islam emphasizes individual accountability for one's actions, sins, and salvation, unlike the Christian belief in the transfer of sin effects to others, which is as unjust.

Moreover, Islam's legitimacy is further supported by how its teachings steer individuals toward virtuous conduct. While other religions may advocate against theft and deceit, their teachings lack practical application.

The most compelling proofs of Islam's authenticity centers around the miraculous nature of the Glorious Quran. Numerous reasons abound to establish the legitimacy of the Glorious Quran as the authentic Word of God. An in-depth analysis of the Glorious Quran leaves no doubt that no one, including the Prophet Muhammad (PBUH), could have authored this Book, as no human could produce anything of its scope and magnitude. Thus, this text could come only from God.

The Glorious Quran serves as the pinnacle of divine miracles, housing thousands of miracles that substantiate its divine inception within it. Claiming to be the verbatim Word of God is a statement of utmost gravity. Without clear evidence or one contradiction in the Book, the apparent Word of God would be proven false. The Glorious Quran, however, remains devoid of contradictions or factual inaccuracies, bolstering its credibility as the Divine Word.

Among the myriad miracles in the Glorious Quran, its unparalleled quality and eloquence shine brightly when read in Arabic. Native Arabic speakers can readily perceive the linguistic mastery embodied in the Glorious Quran—a dynamic testament to the living miracle of the Arabic language. The Arabs who lived at the time of Prophet Muhammad (PBUH) could appreciate the eloquence of the language of the Book, given their familiarity with Arabic.

The Glorious Quran reaches the zenith of linguistic artistry, a standard that defies the realm of human capacity. Flawless grammar graces its pages. Even intricate legal topics, such as inheritance, are explained with vivid imagery in Arabic. Its style, structure, and spiritual resonance are unmatched in the literary world. The Glorious Quran employs terms and descriptions beyond what a 7th-century desert dweller would know.

The Glorious Quran contains many miracles that non-Arabic speakers can appreciate and recognize. Its miraculous impact extends globally, touching millions daily, bringing transformative change, and fostering human betterment. The Glorious Quran possesses an extraordinary spiritual potency, evoking profound emotions and tears in readers, even if they do not speak or comprehend Arabic. Its influence on human history takes various forms, cementing its miraculous nature.

Embedded within the Glorious Quran are references to various branches of knowledge and sciences beyond the grasp of Prophet Muhammad (PBUH) and his contemporaries.

Among the many miracles of the Glorious Quran are hundreds of scientific facts listed in the book, later confirmed to be accurate years after the Book was revealed to a Prophet in the 7th century, who was unlettered in a desert devoid of modern tools. Whereas the Glorious Quran contains accounts of hundreds of scientific miracles, it is not a book of science nor a book of engineering or medicine. The Glorious Quran is a Book of Guidance containing signs that prove its divinity from a higher power.

Among the many notable examples concerns the Glorious Quran's portrayal of human embryonic development within the maternal womb. Describing the growing embryo as "that which hangs," the Glorious Quran anticipates medical knowledge unavailable at the time. It systematically outlines the embryo's progression in three stages and the presence of three protective layers. Modern embryology confirms these Quranic insights. Beyond 7th-century understanding, such intricate details point to the Quran's divine source.

"And certainly did We create man from an extract of clay. Then We placed him as a sperm-drop in a firm lodging. Then We made the sperm-drop into a clinging clot, and We made the clot into a lump of flesh, and We made from the lump, bones, and We covered the bones with flesh; then We developed him into another creation. So blessed is Allah, the best of creators."
(Quran 23:12-14)

Among the Glorious Quran's myriad miracles stands God's declaration that He created all things from water. This Revelation predates the microscopic discovery that life forms predominantly contain water. Today, we understand that cells, the building blocks of life, consist mainly of water.

"…and made from water every living thing?
Then will they not believe?" (Quran 21:30)

In the Glorious Quran, when God speaks of His creations, He often employs the terms "He Created" or "We Created." This "We" signifies the royal we—a singular Creator, not a plural. When referencing iron, the Glorious Quran states it was "sent down" rather than "created". Modern science corroborates this finding, which reveals that the iron that makes up the Earth's core did not come from the Earth itself, but rather from objects in space such as meteorites and stellar explosions billions of years ago.

"Indeed, We sent Our messengers with clear proofs, and with them We sent down the Scripture and the balance of justice so that people may administer justice. And We sent down iron with its great might, benefits for humanity, and means for Allah to prove who is willing to stand up for Him and His messengers without seeing Him. Surely Allah is All-Powerful, Almighty."
(Quran 57:25)

Humans initially thought that the world was flat. The Glorious Quran references the Earth in a verse using the word *dahaha,* a word rooted in the Arabic description for the ostrich egg, remarkably akin to Earth's geo-spherical shape. Furthermore, the word *dahaha* also means *to expand* in Arabic. So, through the use of this word, God tells us that the Earth is ever-expanding, a notion later confirmed to be true.

"And after that He spread the Earth." (Quran 79:30)

When people initially thought that the moon casts its own light, the Glorious Quran references that the moon's light is borrowed or reflected, not inherent—a fact now supported by science since we know that the moon does not generate its own light as the sun does. Instead, the moon reflects the light of the sun, which is why we see it shining in the night sky. In contrast, the Bible's statement in *Genesis 1:16* that the moon is a "lesser light" could be interpreted as implying its own light, a misconception that does not align with scientific understanding.

"Blessed is He who has placed in the sky great stars and placed therein a burning lamp and luminous moon." (Quran 25:61)

Moreover, the Glorious Quran presents the concept of mountains as stabilizing elements for the Earth, using the word *aw'ta'da* in Arabic, which means pegs and stakes, much like those objects that secure a tent. This accurately reflects the role of mountains in anchoring the Earth's crust and maintaining its stability, preventing the Earth from shaking.

"And He has cast into the Earth firmly set mountains, lest it shift with you, and made rivers and roads, that you may be guided."
(Quran 15:15)

Another remarkable miracle in the Glorious Quran is the dialogue attributed to a queen ant warning her fellow ants about impending dangers. We later discovered that ants engage in intricate interactions, including communication, like human communities. Queen ants, serving as central figures in their colonies, communicate and issue instructions to their ant companions. These behaviors reflect a level of organization and complexity akin to human societies.

"Until, when they came upon the valley of the ants, an ant said, 'O ants, enter your dwellings that you not be crushed by Solomon and his soldiers while they perceive not.'" (Quran 27:18)

During Prophet Muhammad's (PBUH) efforts to convey God's Message to the idol-worshippers of Mecca, many rejected his teachings and demanded a miraculous sign to validate his prophethood. They asked for the moon to split as proof, a feat only possible with divine intervention. Prophet Muhammad (PBUH) agreed, and with God's help, the moon briefly split and rejoined. Despite this remarkable event, some remained defiant due to their arrogance and refused to accept his prophethood.

"The Hour of Judgment is nigh, and the moon is cleft asunder. And if they behold a portent they turn away and say: Prolonged illusion. They denied the truth and followed their own lusts. Yet everything will come to a decision." (Quran 54:1)

In today's era of advanced technology, NASA has provided visual evidence through a captured image that cracks exist on the moon's surface, indicating that it had split and later rejoined. This aligns with historical accounts from Prophet Muhammad's companions present during the event. Additionally, even accounts from those who were opposed to Prophet Muhammad (PBUH) confirm the occurrence of the moon splitting. Reports from various geographical locations, including India, provide independent testimonies of witnessing this phenomenon. These records raise a significant question.

I've highlighted only a handful of the numerous scientific miracles in the Glorious Quran. A quick internet search will unveil the multitude of other astonishing revelations it holds. The question naturally arises: How could an illiterate man living in the desert during that era possess such remarkably advanced knowledge unless it was directly bestowed from a divine source?

Yet, the Glorious Quran's miracles extend beyond linguistics and science; It also contains prophecies and predictions concerning future events that have undeniably materialized, further proving its divine origin.

Among the many remarkable predictions that grace its pages, the Glorious Quran includes a bold assertion about the victory of the Byzantine Empire over the Persian Empire. This prophetic statement was made in the early 7th century when these two empires held sway as dominant global powers engaged in a fierce rivalry. The Byzantines suffered a severe defeat in their fight against the Persians at the time, which seemed to doom the Empire. Yet, the Glorious Quran confidently foretold their eventual victory within three to nine years. Within that timeframe, the Byzantine Empire defeated the Persian Empire, a development that defied all expectations.

In this context, the Almighty proclaims:

"The Byzantines have been defeated. In the nearest land. But they, after their defeat, will overcome. Within three to nine years. To Allah belongs the command before and after. And that day the believers will rejoice. In the victory of Allah. He gives victory to whom He wills, and He is the Exalted in Might, the Merciful."
(Quran 30: 2-5)

Indeed, this prophetic insight not only came to fruition but also remarkably detailed that the Romans' defeat occurred in the lowest part of the Earth. Astonishingly, modern satellite imagery confirms the location of their defeat corresponds to the lowest point on Earth, about 400 meters below sea level.

The Pharaoh, who lived in the time of Prophet Moses (PBUH), had power and wealth; he even arrogantly proclaimed himself God. His ultimate downfall resulted from his arrogance, culminating in his drowning. In a verse within the Glorious Quran, God declared that He would preserve the body of the Pharaoh as a testament for future generations. The Pharaoh's body was discovered in 1898.

In the early '70s, his corpse was examined. It was discovered through intense investigation of his mummy that he had died from direct water infiltration into his lung, providing conclusive proof of a drowning death. It also was proven that he lived at the time of the Prophet Moses (PBUH). God preserved his body forever as a sign and lesson for humanity, as He had promised in His Final Revelation. This body is displayed in a museum and often tours the world for everyone to see.

"So today We will save you in body that you may be to those who succeed you a sign. And indeed, many among the people, of Our signs, are heedless." (Quran 10:92)

Many other prophecies fill the Glorious Quran; for instance, God states he will preserve and protect His final Revelation to humanity, the Glorious Quran, from any form of human alteration or corruption. As previously mentioned, the Glorious Quran has remained unaltered, retaining its original wording to the last letter.

"Indeed, it is We who sent down the message [i.e., the Quran], and indeed, We will be its guardian." (Quran 15:9)

Additionally, the Glorious Quran declares that God has made it easily memoizable, a claim validated by the fact that hundreds of thousands of individuals worldwide have committed the entire Book to memory, encompassing over 600 pages. This feat has been achieved by millions of people, regardless of their age, ethnicities and languages.

"And indeed We have already made the Quran easy for remembrance. Are there any that will recollect?" (Quran 54:17)

The prophetic sayings of Prophet Muhammad (PBUH), known as Hadith, also have conveyed many predictions. One such prophecy stated by our Prophet (PBUH) is that a time will come when the children of barefooted camel and goat herders will participate in the construction of high-rise buildings. The prophecy was made when the Arabs were not known for building tall buildings like the Romans, Greeks, and Egyptians, and there were no indications that Arabs would construct tall buildings given that they were living as impoverished herders of camels and sheep.

However, Prophet Muhammad (PBUH) predicted that the Arabs would one day surpass these civilizations in architectural achievement. This prophecy is now being fulfilled, as Arabs are participating in constructing high-rise buildings—as sign that the day if judgement is near according to our Prophet PBUH.

The fathers of the current rulers of Dubai and Saudi Arabia once walked barefoot and worked primarily as herders of camels and goats before discovering oil. Today, Dubai and Saudi Arabia host the world's tallest buildings. *And when you see barefoot, naked, destitute shepherds constructing tall buildings... – Saheeh Muslim*

The Prophet Muhammad (PBUH) also foretold the conquest of Jerusalem after his passing, its subsequent loss, and eventual recapture. He prophesied the conquest of Persia, Rome, and Egypt, all unfolding as he predicted. Following his departure, Muslims conquered Constantinople (now Istanbul), fulfilling another prophecy. He also predicted the global expansion of Islam to both the Eastern and Western extremities of the world, a vision now realized as Islam spans across the globe, encompassing around 24% of the global population.

Among the many predictions of Prophet Muhammad (PBUH) is the claim that a time would come when "...*women are clothed yet naked, walking with an enticing gait...*" (*Saheeh Muslim*). Today, women worldwide walk in the streets with many body parts exposed, flaunting their beauty as the Hadith had predicted.

Prophet Muhammed (PBUH) prophesied a time when murders would increase; the one who kills would not know why they killed, nor would the one killed understand the motive. One can see this phenomenon happening in modern wars and gang-related conflicts.

Prophet Muhammed (PBUH) prophesied the increase in usury and interest, unethical and exploitative acts as they make the rich richer at the expense of the poor. He stated that no one could escape this state, which, unfortunately, defines the world's current economic conditions.

The Glorious Quran also shares stories from the past about different nations and prophets like Joseph, Moses, and Jesus (PBUT). The Prophet Muhammad (PBUH) lived in a desert area without libraries and grew up among illiterate idol worshippers without knowledge of the Scriptures.

He had no way of reading or conjuring these stories shared in the Glorious Quan.

"That is from the news of the unseen which We reveal to you, [O Muhammad]. You knew it not, neither you nor your people, before this. So be patient; indeed, the best outcome is for the righteous." (Quran 11:49)

God taught the Glorious Quran to the Angel Gabriel, who then passed it on to the Prophet Muhammad (PBUH). He, in turn, taught it to his companions. It's important to note that Muslims recorded this Revelation as it was conveyed to them by the Prophet Muhammad (PBUH) over a span of 23 years. The Glorious Quran was revealed orally, not in written form. Once compiled, it became evident that the Glorious Quran has a profound mathematical structure and design beyond human achievement. The Glorious Quran contains numerous mathematical patterns or connections that appear more than mere coincidences.

One of the mathematical wonders of the Quran is the number of repetitions of certain words, which indicates a deliberate intention behind it. For example, the word "day" is used 365 times, which is the duration of the Earth's orbit around the sun. The word "month" is mentioned 12 times, and the words "man" and "woman" are each mentioned 24 times. The terms "Dunya" (referring to our present world) and "Hereafter" are both mentioned 115 times.

Once again, the Glorious Quran was not revealed all at once. Instead, it was gradually disclosed to Prophet Muhammad (PBUH) by Angel Gabriel over 23 years, addressing specific events and questions the Prophet didn't have immediate answers to. The notion that a human could compile the Glorious Quran, enriched with numerous mathematical marvels within this timeframe, seems implausible. These examples I've shared are just a glimpse of the countless miracles woven into the fabric of the Glorious Quran. These miracles, among others, underscore a purposeful arrangement within the Glorious Quran. The various mathematical patterns observed cannot be mere coincidences.

In contrast to the modern-day Bible, which has accumulated thousands of contradictions due to numerous alterations, the Glorious Quran stands out for its impeccable consistency, free from contradictions.

"Then do they not reflect upon the Qur'an? If it had been from any other than Allah, they would have found within it much contradiction." (Quran 4:82)

The Glorious Quran challenges those questioning its Divine source to produce another sacred text or even a Chapter of equal caliber that matches its eloquence, power, style, and language. Even though the shortest Chapter in the Glorious Quran is three Verses long, Allah unequivocally states that no one will be capable of producing a chapter like anything on par with the Glorious Quran—a prediction found within the Glorious Quran that has proven to be accurate.

"And if you are in doubt about what We have sent down upon Our Servant [Muhammad], then produce a Surah (Chapter) the like thereof and call upon your witnesses other than Allah, if you should be truthful" (Quran 2:23)

You carry an instinctive inclination to believe in and worship your Creator, who is one without partners. This belief isn't the result of learned knowledge or personal contemplation; instead, it's a core element infused by God into every human heart. Over time, this innate belief may be influenced and muddled by changing surroundings and external influences from family and friends. As Prophet Muhammad (PBUH) conveyed, *"Every child is born in a state of fitrah (natural belief in God), then his parents make him a Jew, a Christian, or a Magian." (Saheeh Muslim)*

You were born with an inherent curiosity and capacity to seek out your Creator, to acknowledge and comprehend the existence of God. When many uncover the truthfulness of Islam, they eagerly embrace it, surrendering themselves entirely to their Creator's will—a path you should follow as well.

If uncertainty lingers regarding your decision to embrace Islam, you can direct your prayers to God without explicitly mentioning His name. Offer your supplication by saying, *"Oh, You who created me, please guide me to the truth."* Then, continue to research and look further into the overwhelming evidence and proof that Islam and the Glorious Quran offer to affirm its existence and validity. Do not procrastinate, and do not take this matter of faith lightly, as you are not guaranteed a tomorrow! Your life test can end at any moment. Realize that you did not come to this randomly or by chance, my dear brother or sister; your Creator has guided you here.

www.ingramcontent.com/pod-product-compliance
Lightning Source LLC
Chambersburg PA
CBHW051652120626
46551CB00015B/2321